Quantity discounts are available from the publisher:

BAUDVILLE, INC.
5380 52nd Street SE
Grand Rapids, MI 49512

1.800.728.0888
www.baudville.com

Priceless
Motivation

*Quick tips to excite and inspire
your most valuable asset...*

People!

Cover, interior design and illustrations by Joseph L. Naimo

Research, content and material supplied by Kim Smithson, Incentive Automation LLC

Text adapted by Estelle Slootmaker

Produced by Debra Sikanas

Quotations used in this book are from public sources and do not imply endorsement.

Table of Contents

Priceless Words quoted from

Andy Grove, Intel Corporation; Mary Kay Ash, Mary Kay Cosmetics; Jerry McAdams, Maritz Information Resources; Wilfred Peterson, *The Art of Living* ; Scudder Parker; American Psycholinguistic Research Society, Joan P. Klubnik, *Rewarding & Recognizing Employees*; and others

ISBN 0-930393-78-3

I

Mission: Recognition

People count
(and... people count on recognition)

Throughout time and across cultural boundaries, people of all ages have always valued recognition. We all need it, crave it and respond to it. At the core of any energized, productive group, you'll find recognition of effort and achievement, acknowledgment of a job well done. While *Priceless Motivation* focuses on recognition in the corporate world, the recognition programs herein can add a positive dynamic to any environment: at work and play, in school or church, in the annals of government or in the comfort of your own home.

Corporate success and top performance do not happen by accident. It takes planning, preparation, investment and commitment. Recognition programs require the same insights. We're not talking about carrots on the ends of sticks. We're inviting you to be human, to buy into the one central philosophy of true success:

People are the lifeblood of your business. By valuing and recognizing them, you harness the power of motivation. That's the single, most powerful strategy you can use to promote performance. In any company, managers want motivated people — people who get

Priceless Words

"All a manager can do is create an environment in which motivated people can flourish."

Andy Grove, Intel Corporation

1

Priceless Words

According to a recently published Sales & Marketing Management poll of Fortune 1000 companies, the number one reason people leave their jobs is lack of praise and recognition.

Priceless Deeds

The sweet taste of success

A sales manager for an auto parts manufacturer brought in a giant chocolate chip cookie to his staff when they had met their quarterly sales target. The words "Ah, The Sweet Taste of Success" were written in frosting on top of the cookie. This surprising treat was the hit of the sales meeting.

the job done and offer ideas on how to do the job better. Read the classified ads — the job descriptions all cry out for "self-motivated doers." Unfortunately, filling your ranks with self-motivated people isn't enough. Even the most self-motivated person loses the spark in a negative — or benign — environment where they aren't recognized for their contributions.

Motivation can't be whipped up in the corporate kitchen and benevolently force-fed to people. Like the other grand human emotions, you can't make people feel it. Motivation comes from within. However, external sources can indirectly affect a person's feelings of being motivated. By recognizing accomplishments, building self-esteem and being sensitive to individual qualities, we can kindle the sparks of motivation that lie within.

Recognize good work, reward successful results

The concept is simple… ask any successful parent or school teacher. Rewarding a good behavior reinforces it, and makes it more likely to be repeated. Adults aren't a whole lot different. When you reward a good attempt or successful result, you let people know what's really important to the company. Your actions speak louder than the words written in the company handbook or mission statement. By rewarding and recognizing employees, you clarify what behaviors and outcomes you value most. (It boils down to telling people what you really want.)

For example, if customer service tops your list, tell workers what it looks like: "Customer service means resolving the customer's issues on the spot and with a smile. Go the extra mile! Exert a positive attitude and cheerful disposition!" When you see people practice what you've preached, praise them. Reward them. You'll see it become a habit.

CUSTOMER SERVICE
AWARD

This award is presented to
CHARLES HOLT
for outstanding performance in Customer Service.
Your efforts reflect a good image on all of us at
Custom Communications

When promotions, raises and rewards consistently go to your movers and shakers – the people generating new ideas, innovative methods, proactive solutions and extra effort — everyone gets the message: you sincerely value excellence and ongoing improvement. In other words, it makes sense to walk your talk. Reward your shining stars.

Priceless Pointer

Employee-to-employee thank you's

Recognition doesn't always have to come from manager to employee. In fact, some of the most effective recognition comes from among co-workers. When your co-workers excel, write a note, have a little chat expressing thanks, send an e-mail or give a kind word of encouragement. Any of these can be a great motivating force.

3

Build individual attitudes, boost group morale

Among other benefits, recognition programs improve attitudes and morale. An attitude is owned by a single person; morale is the collection of a group of attitudes. By improving individual attitudes, the overall morale improves. Managers need to realize that both are by-products of recognizing people's accomplishments and tuning into their individual needs.

Touching people's lives

Recognition done right takes sincerity — a personal touch. To be memorable and meaningful, you have to touch people's lives. A heartfelt compliment, a sincere thank you, recognition at a meeting, a handwritten note, a certificate of appreciation or a symbolic gesture say more than any amount of flamboyant glitz. Whatever your style, show your appreciation on a consistent basis — whenever people do the job right.

Have you ever heard management say something like, "I don't have to say thank you. That's her job," or, "He can like it or lump it." Such a defensive posture is really a "mini-temper tantrum" and rarely creates a positive response. While deadline pressures seem to leave little time for recognition, the kind word or thoughtful deed may give that employee the extra 'oomph' he or she needed to complete the job on time.

While job descriptions make a good starting point, people regard the daily grind as their real job description. When someone goes above and beyond — does something you want to see more of — it's only rational

Priceless Words

"It's up to you to decide how to speak to your people. Do you single out individuals for public praise and recognition? Make people who work for you feel important? If you honor and serve them, they'll honor and serve you."

Mary Kay Ash,
Mary Kay Cosmetics

thinking to recognize and reward the occasion. By reinforcing such an accomplishment with recognition, you lock-in improvement. "Above and beyond" becomes a matter of course.

Small starts

You don't have to redesign this year's budget to start a recognition program. Start with small courtesies. We all like to be appreciated.

- A compliment
- An ice cream cone
- A sticker
- A handwritten thank you
- A certificate of appreciation
- A helping hand
- A personal note
- A day off
- A smile
- Recognition at a meeting
- A pat on the back
- An article in the company newsletter
- Two words said with sincerity, "Thank you"

Priceless Deeds

This bud's for you!

Ann, an administrative assistant to the vice president of sales for a large pharmaceutical company, had won several service awards. The one she remembers best came after struggling through a grueling month of sales overload during the busy season. After putting in extra hours for more than two weeks, Ann's boss presented her with a red carnation and a thank you note that read: "Thanks for everything! This bud's for you." Ann pressed the flower and has kept it ever since. Ann shares, "It was a little thing that made a big difference."

Priceless Deeds

Candid Camera

A flood disaster struck over the weekend in a small southern town, damaging a large mail-order distribution facility. Employees rushed in to help. When things were back to normal, the company sponsored a catered lunch for the whole crew to recognize all their efforts. The manager made an oversized collage, thank you card for the lunchroom with assorted pictures he had snapped during the cleanup. In addition, he gave all the workers individual thank you cards with individual snapshots of each person during the cleanup.

Gain impact with feedback

- Give feedback as often as possible
- Give feedback as soon as possible
- If it's bad news, add a spoonful of sugar

Positive feedback impacts people's attitudes and helps make high achievement a habit. Achievement is at the heart of making employees feel good about their work — and their company. Achievement brings a sense of worth to the individual and success in the marketplace.

As a token given for accomplishment, a reward denotes success with an ongoing task, a key program or continuing job. A reward symbolizes a job well done over time. Unlike a sporting event that starts with a whistle and ends with one winner, our jobs are ongoing and repetitive. A reward fixes a point in time and commemorates an achievement. Rewards give a sense of "winning the game."

Reward milestone results with celebrated fanfare. The actual reward should be tied to effective performance, be appropriate for the recipient and reflect corporate objectives. Present rewards as soon as possible after the achievement; this will help inspire continuing success. Tailoring the reward to the recipient's personality makes it more meaningful. A generic certificate hastily stamped with a signature won't do much to motivate. However, a thoughtfully designed certificate specifically describing the achievement, signed by the manager — or better yet — the whole team, and presented in a lovely commemorative folder will brim with meaning. Why? Because you took the time.

Incentive and recognition products that tie into an organization's goals provide a memorable sense of closure and common sense that, perhaps, a toaster presented in appreciation of insurance policy sales simply would not communicate. Instead, if the salesperson was known to be a runner, present a personalized Extra Mile Award certificate along with a gift certificate for a pair of running shoes.

Priceless Deeds

Several years ago, Telcorp, a communications company, instituted their "Make A Positive Difference" recognition program. Managers nominated employees who made significant positive contributions to their business unit for consideration by a committee. During monthly unit meetings, managers recognized their recipients with a handwritten card signed by the president, a commemorative gold medallion and a $50 donation to the charity of their choice.

PART I
Summing up...

- *People Count – they're the lifeblood of your business*

- *Recognition harnesses the power of motivation*

- *Recognition builds good attitudes in individuals and improvement in company-wide morale*

- *Recognition proves more meaningful and memorable when it's personal*

- *Start with small courtesies and positive feedback*

- *Praising performance brings a sense of worth to the individual and success in the marketplace*

Inventive Incentives

Winning Awards

Stimulate outward performance, fuel inner drive

While you may hear the words used interchangeably, *incentive* and *recognition* have very different meanings. Both reward and motivate performance. However, they do so quite differently. An incentive drives performance like a contract. An if/then clause establishes expected performance for a promised reward: "Do this, get that." Recognition fuels the inner drive, igniting the spark of self-motivation into a fully-energized flame of continuing accomplishment.

Incentives

Incentives reward results with external benefits such as pay, promotions, benefits or office space. For example, you offer people a percentage of the money saved by a suggestion they've made. Or, when your salespeople reach a certain dollar goal, you reward them with a Caribbean cruise. These "extrinsic" incentives motivate people to work a little harder than usual. Because incentives reward performance or results, they are usually self-funding. No results — no rewards. So, incentives are often the most cost-effective, results-effective and risk-free form of compensation.

Priceless Deeds

Monetary Bonuses

In 1994, Blue Cross and Blue Shield of Massachusetts developed their Team Incentive Program. Each employee team works with their team leader to establish goals. At year's end, the team compares its actual performance with their stated goals. A sliding scale bonus of up to 7 percent of their base pay rewards successful team members, depending on how well the team reached its objectives.

From "Motivating for Success"
Sales & Marketing Strategies & News
May 6, 1997

SALES AWARD

Presented with gratitude to
JASON T. MALDOON II
whose marketing magnetism,
creative cunning, and sales superiority
have helped make us all more successful.

November 25

EMPLOYEE OF THE MONTH

Presented to

PAUL ROBERTS

with our gratitude for your
outstanding performance.

Recognition

While people do enjoy extra money and added perks, many receive greater satisfaction from knowing someone valued their contributions. This "intrinsic" motivation drives people to perform for an internal sense of accomplishment. Many a manager or CEO may say, "Well, my people should work hard. That's what they're paid for. "But how will people know they're doing a good job if we don't tell them? Recognition lets them know.

Priceless Deeds

Positive Reinforcement

Boardroom, Inc. implemented an Ideas Power program that gives positive reinforcement to employees when they come up with ideas — no matter how small. Initially, the program rewarded employees with dollar bills and candy bars. The rewards now range from $5 or $10 for single ideas to $50 for the most good ideas in a month.

"Firms' Little Rewards Can Spawn Big Ideas"

Chicago Tribune, Sunday, February 11, 1996

Your well-constructed recognition program will help you...

- Meet people's needs for achievement and recognition
- Translate company values into specific work habits
- Focus efforts on achieving specific goals
- Achieve profitability and growth
- Create a culture where people really want to do their best
- Tell people what's really important to the organization
- Improve individual attitudes
- Boost overall morale
- Produce role models for future programs
- Commemorate achievement with a sense of accomplishment and closure
- Foster healthy competition between

individuals and teams

• Create loyal, committed employees

As an after-the-fact display of appreciation for a contribution, recognition often surprises the recipient (who performed well for reasons other than receiving recognition). By addressing the individual's need for self-esteem and belonging, recognition bestows strong intrinsic rewards. Where incentives emphasize specific behavior leading to desired results, recognition expresses feelings of pride and camaraderie, in both the person giving the recognition and the person receiving it.

Recognition has lasting, residual effects on the rest of the organization. The material award, often minimal in extrinsic value, becomes an important symbol of management's sincerity and commitment to corporate values and culture. In this manner, recognition significantly impacts morale and performance. Most people want to do a good job and are willing to work hard. But, they need direction in what they do and feedback on how they're doing it. Recognition provides feedback while building self-esteem and inner drive.

When people are routinely recognized for their efforts, they begin to trust in the system, knowing that their hard work will be rewarded. They become more committed to their organization. Incentives, when used in tandem with recognition, can ignite a synergy that empowers the individual and the organization.

Priceless Deeds

Whirlpool Corporation of Benton Harbor, Michigan, instituted the Performance Management Process in 1989. The company bases annual payouts on a combination of corporate performance and individual employee performance.

"Motivating For Success"
Sales & Marketing Strategies & News
May 6, 1997

Team Player Award

This certificate hereby grants
Darleen Roberts
Honor and Distinction as the employee of
EXCELL SALES GROUP
who best exemplifies the team concept.

Doug Moore
Doug Moore

Bill Prescott
Bill Prescott

Priceless Pointer

Incentives vs. Recognition

An incentive is a contract with an if/then clause that promises a reward for specific action: "Do this, get that."

Recognition is an after-the-fact display of appreciation for a job well done.

In public and private, recognition works for you

Highly visible, public recognition calls attention to a person's achievement in a group setting — at a meeting or conference, in a newsletter or over the intercom. More intimate, private recognition takes place one-on-one, for example, between the manager and employee — a thank-you note, an e-mail, a praising chat in your office. Competitive extroverts thrive more on public recognition, while quiet, introverts might prefer a private, informal recognition. Be sensitive to individuals' differences. Take time to get to know them informally so you can meet their needs. If you're not sure, ask — either in private conversation or with a questionnaire.

What does recognition look like?

Recognition has many faces. It can be a social acknowledgment for a job done well — a pat on the back, a verbal thank you, a praise. Such positive recognition creates positive feelings. Reward people when they demonstrate performance above what's expected… when an employee covers for a sick co-worker or when a team completes a project ahead of schedule. Practice praise repeatedly with repeat performers. Like recognition, praise motivates people to reach new levels of achievement.

Material rewards include tangible objects like certificates, money, benefits, travel, entertainment or personal service awards. Tangible rewards back up social acknowledgments. However, using material rewards too frequently or inappropriately can make people feel manipulated. Conversely, when you use social acknowledgment exclusively, and never with a tangible reward, people may feel like your praise is empty and meaningless. The most successful recognition programs recognize people with both praise and material rewards.

The 3-to-1 Rule

While no universal, magical formula for every scenario exists, a good mix of social acknowledgment and tangible reward follows the 3-to-1 Rule: when people have consistently performed at or above expectations, and you have rewarded their performance with a social acknowledgment three times, recognize the next great performance with a tangible reward to commemorate their excellent achievements.

Here's the 3-to-1 Rule in action. In January, Mary Jo stayed late an entire week to finish an important report. Her boss, John, stopped her in the hall after her presentation, told her she had done an extremely thorough job, said she had been very well prepared for the presentation, and congratulated her on her efforts (SOCIAL ACKNOWLEDGMENT #1).

In February, Mary Jo helped John prepare a speech he had to make at a local Chamber event. The speech went well. John wrote Mary Jo a note thanking her for her contribution (SOCIAL ACKNOWLEDGMENT #2).

Priceless Deeds

The traveling bronze shoe

Rose, a hospital administrator, got tired of hearing bickering among the various departments. They argued about budgets and duties, and pointed fingers when things went wrong. Turnover was impossibly high. Rose decided to take action when her beleaguered assistant suggested, "Everyone should walk around in my shoes for awhile."

"That's it," Rose thought. "People need to walk in other people's shoes to understand the issues they face."

Rose developed an awareness program with a traveling trophy: a large, bronzed shoe. When people presented solutions or worked together as a team, they were the caretakers of the large, bronzed shoe until it got passed along.

Priceless Pointer

Recognize extraordinary achievement in ordinary duties

- Inventory control
- Cash management
- R & D
- Defect reduction
- On-the-job safety
- Punctuality
- Loyalty
- Positive Attitude
- Attendance

In April, Mary Jo made several popular suggestions in a group meeting on product development. John called attention to Mary's ideas in the group and recognized her creativity (SOCIAL ACKNOWLEDGMENT #3).

By June, Mary Jo's team had a working prototype of the new product she had proposed in April — developed in record time. John took Mary Jo out to lunch to discuss her ideas and recognize her achievement. He also told her that he wanted to do something to recognize her hard work over the past six months. He knew she was moving to a new apartment soon, so he offered her a three-day weekend for the date of her choice (TANGIBLE AWARD).

What does this example say about recognition? First, you should spread recognition over time. Performance rarely concentrates in mere days or even weeks. This real-world example shows that effective recognition can be public or private — or both. Also, it shows recognition coming from management (Mary Jo's boss) as the most effective kind of recognition. John doesn't wait until a month after the fact; he always recognizes Mary Jo's efforts right after the performance occurs. Finally, to be meaningful, recognition must be personal. When John takes Mary Jo to lunch, he gives her a personal audience, a forum for her thoughts and ideas. As a tuned-in employer, he realizes that an extra day off would be of great help to her in her move. He offers the day off as a reward for both her immediate efforts and the culmination of efforts during the last six months.

A quick-start recognition program

So, where do you start? Building recognition into your organization won't happen overnight. If the supervisors and managers in your company haven't been doing it all along, if it isn't a part of your corporate culture already, you'll need to start with the basics.

1. Listen to people

2. Look for opportunities to recognize them

3. Praise them for their work

Listen

First, managers must learn to listen to the people they work with. Simply listening to employees' perspectives on company problems, ideas and issues makes people feel valued. People become motivated when managers take the time to consider their input. To be a better listener, establish eye-contact, take notes and ask questions. Show you're truly interested in what's being said. Active listening tells people that their input is important… and they are important.

Look

Next, managers must make a conscious effort to look for recognition opportunities. You may have a million items on your to-do list, deadlines to meet and projects to finish. Even so, take a few seconds to stop and look at the activity around

Priceless Words

"Reward people along the way. Success is not arriving at the summit of a mountain as a final destination. It is a continuing upward spiral of progress."

Wilfred Peterson,
The Art of Living

you. Instead of waiting for the problems and mistakes to find you, go out and look for the achievements and successes. By focusing on what goes on around you, you will become more aware of the qualities that make your organization work: teamwork, cooperation, communication and people. At first, you'll have to stop and make time to look for these golden opportunities for recognition. After awhile, it will become second nature. If you want to change the culture of your company… if you want to create a positive environment… if you want a staff of motivated, energized workers… make a commitment to look for rewardable activity. This is the single most important step you can take.

Praise

Keep it simple for starters. Follow the 3-to-1 Rule of praise: reward the first three instances of excellent performance with a social acknowledgment (a pat on the back, a compliment, a thank-you note) and the next one with a tangible reward (an award certificate, lunch or a day off).

Why praise?

Praise reinforces, recognizes and motivates desirable behavior. When you praise people, you make people feel good about themselves and good about their jobs. Almost magically, attitude improves and morale is bolstered. The best is yet to come… these recognized, motivated people will prove to be the most productive people around.

Go public...

- In meetings
- At conferences
- During company gatherings
- In your newsletters
- As correspondence to customers
- On your organization's web site
- Via news releases
- On billboards
- Through associations
- With framed certificates

... or keep it under wraps

- Write it in a thank you card
- Share it during a performance review
- Say it in person
- Key it via e-mail
- Send a message home via mail

Priceless Words

"Psycholinguistic research indicates a person's mind takes 48% longer to understand a negative statement than a positive one. Thus compliments become a dynamic force in motivating others."

American Psycholinguistic Research Society

Priceless Deeds

Catch Them Doing Something Right

Jack Conway, general manager of Exel Inn in Appleton, Wisconsin, uses a "Catch Them Doing Something Right" approach to recognition and praise. When Jack notices people going above and beyond the call of duty, or when a customer compliments good service, he singles out the employee for a praise — whenever possible, on the spot, in front of the customer or other employees. He also keeps tangible rewards on hand to give out spontaneously: gift certificates from local restaurants, quick oil change garages or grocery stores. "Immediacy is the key. When people perform and perform well, I want to praise them on the spot," says Conway.

The four key qualities

An effective praise is:

Sincere

People sense sincerity and commitment a mile away. Sarcasm or a flip attitude will undermine your message and do more harm than good.

Immediate

For the greatest effect, praise should occur as soon after the event as possible. Praising someone a month after the performance isn't nearly as effective as just after the fact.

Specific

Saying, "Good job on the report," won't work as well as, "I really appreciate your attention to detail on the report you did for me last week. The facts were clear and it was error free. Thanks for your effort."

Meaningful

Meaningful praise ties the praise back to an individual's personality or qualities. "I really appreciate your attention to detail on the report you did for me last week. The facts were clear and it was error free. It's great having such a thorough, dependable person on staff."

PART II
Summing up...

- *Extrinsic incentives reward results with material gains, such as money or prizes*

- *Most people receive greater satisfaction from knowing they're valued*

- *Recognition bestows intrinsic rewards, such as self-esteem and a sense of belonging*

- *Used together, incentives and recognition can ignite a synergy that empowers the individual and the organization*

Start your recognition program with the basics:

- *Listen to people*

- *Look for opportunities to recognize them*

- *Praise them for their work*

People pleasin' praise is Sincere, Immediate, Specific and Meaningful.

Shining Examples

Winning rewards to motivate your star performers

As we talked about previously, praise presents social acknowledgment while a reward bestows a tangible, material "trophy." For the best results, your recognition program should strategically combine the two. Your choice of rewards will depend in part on the specific accomplishment you are recognizing as well as the type of recognition program you've decided to implement. Different rewards can be effective in different circumstances.

With a little bit of creativity, no-cost and low-cost rewards — such as certificates commemorating good performance or a noteworthy accomplishment — can make a very memorable impression. In other circumstances, money, benefits, merchandise, an evening's entertainment or travel serve well as rewards. By understanding how each of these different rewards work, you can choose the ones that your star performers will value.

Priceless Words

"Recognition is a pulling strategy. Employees experience managers practicing recognition, like the way it feels, and are "pulled" into the process — first as recipients and then as initiators."

Joan P. Klubnik, Rewarding & Recognizing Employees

PERKS with PIZAZZ
"No-cost" rewards... just invest a little imagination

Some of the best rewards are free. For example, wash an associate's car out in the parking lot, change roles for the day, let an employee attend a meeting in your place, give a dedicated worker a new title, designate a VIP parking

25

Priceless Pointer

Don't underestimate the power symbolic gestures have on workers. A little bit of time and a little bit of money can go a long way when recognizing people's contributions.

spot, invite a deserving pet-lover to bring their pooch to the office for the day or let a workaholic leave a few hours early. The possibilities are endless. The key is creativity. With the right spin, a small and simple action becomes a memorable way of saying, "Thanks for all your hard work."

Priced-less perks

Stretch a limited award budget with creative recognition

- Attendance at a seminar
- A magazine subscription
- Membership in a professional organization
- Enrollment in a mentoring program
- A donation to the charity of the person's choice
- Time-off
- A motivational calendar
- A framed print for the office
- A unique computer screen saver

Perks plus personality

Spend some time with your award winner

- Take them out for ice cream
- Spring for lunch or dinner
- Treat them to a show
- Pack a picnic lunch for a nearby park
- Take them shopping
- See some local sights

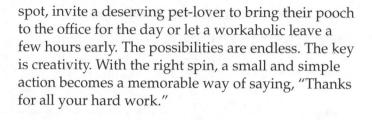

Gift certificates... nice and easy

Having another busy day? This coupon is good for...
ONE EXPRESS-TO-YOUR-DESK LUNCH.
If you're going to work through another lunch, it might as well be filling!

Sign here to accept, return coupon to me

Gift certificates give the added flexibility of choice. Be it from a retailer, specialty store, restaurant, theater or salon, your award winner gets to choose exactly what they want. While sure to please, gift certificates have the downside of being somewhat impersonal. Make them more meaningful by presenting them with a personalized award certificate.

Money talks... but what is it saying?

If you stopped ten people on the street and asked them what was the number one thing that motivated them, probably nine of them would tell you "money." However, though an effective motivator in certain cases, money can become a tricky and unpredictable reward.

How using cash rewards causes problems:

• Money starts to feel like a bribe after awhile

• Dollars deny intrinsic rewards

• People get used to it; it ends up taking more money to get the same result

• Money focuses people's attention on the almighty dollar

When people strive solely for money, they may be tempted to take the shortest route to maximizing their financial gain — even if it means sacrificing quality or service. Because of these limitations, an effective recognition program will either not use money as a reward, or else use it in combination with a more effective reward.

Priceless Deeds

"We're out to the movies: be back in two hours"

Sam operated a small staffing company in Chicago. After a particularly crazy month, tempers were flaring everywhere. On the spur of the moment, Sam closed the office and hung out a homemade sign that said, "We're Out To The Movies: Be Back in Two Hours." He then loaded the entire staff into two vans and took them to see a comedy. People talked about it for months. Sam restored good humor and became company hero as well as boss.

PART III Shining Examples

Priceless Words

"Most Americans say they want more money. Yet non-cash awards appear to be more effective motivators."

Jerry McAdams
Vice President, Maritz Information Resources, 1987

Awards don't have to be big or expensive!

The key is letting people know you appreciate their performance. In turn, they'll feel good about themselves and appreciate your recognition of their efforts. You can express recognition with:

- Candy bars
- Stuffed animals
- A homemade trophy
- Flowers
- A greeting card
- A decorated cake

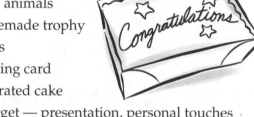

Don't forget — presentation, personal touches and pomp and circumstance make awards more meaningful.

Merchandise that motivates

Another useful tool in your recognition program, merchandise rewards can effectively, and uniquely, motivate your top performers. Artwork, appliances, electronics, home furnishings, sports equipment, apparel, desk accessories, books… how do you choose? Select merchandise that personally relates to your award winner. If you designate John as "Employee of the Month" and you know he loves music, present him with a portable CD Player. And remember, awards must be timely to have impact and meaning. If John was "Employee of the Month" in January and gets his CD Player in April, you'll miss the motivational momentum that comes from timely recognition.

Pamper with a personal service

In today's busy world, one of the most appreciated forms of awards can be for a personal service — maid service for a month, lawn service for a summer, employee financial planning, ten sessions with a personal trainer. Such service awards save people time, energy and effort, typically with chores they would rather not do or with pampering they wouldn't do for themselves. Many times, these personal services are valued far beyond their cost.

Applaud them with entertainment

Everyone enjoys entertainment. Front row seats at a professional ball game, tickets for the theatre or comedy club, a dinner cruise, a movie or dinner out… any of these provide people with enjoyable, memorable experiences that they will talk about for weeks. Often savored and valued (beyond their time), entertainment awards allow people to enjoy an experience that they might not spend their own money on.

Bonus benefits boost morale

While employees view some benefits as entitlements (like health insurance), other benefits can make great rewards for achievements. Nontraditional benefits, like gain sharing, profit sharing, flex-time, and stock

If the award excites them…
it will most likely motivate them!

options are gaining popularity for two reasons. (1) People want these benefits; and (2) performance–based benefits make a great motivator.

Travel – a first-class incentive

Surveys have shown incentive travel as one of the most motivating awards available to participants in an incentive program. The glamour and excitement of exotic locations, fancy hotels, fine dining and first-class travel can drive employees to work harder, longer and faster.

Make it personal with an award certificate

Make any of these reward ideas even more memorable by presenting them along with a personalized award certificate. Mounted in a frame or on a plaque, a certificate proves a cost-effective way to get the most miles out of your motivational moment.

Certificates commemorate achievement in a tangible, personalized format. To be effective, certificates must specifically note the person's achievement, be attractive in design, show quality and care in their construction, and be correct as far as names and dates.

Five tips on recognizing with award certificates

Say it with style

Include your award winner's name, achievement, the date and any other important information about the accomplishment.

Design is everything

Be creative! Choose papers to match the occasion — be it fun and colorful or elegant and serious.

Have an authority endorse it

Ask the company vice president or president to sign the certificate along with the manager and co-workers.

Present it properly

Don't leave a certificate with smeared ink in the employee's mailbox. Choose a quality paper, place it in a presentation folder or frame it… then present it personally. Elegant presentation underscores your appreciation and your recipient's importance.

Dignify the occasion

Present the certificate at a company function or meeting. If your presentation will be one-on-one, make it special by treating your award winner to lunch.

Priceless Pointer

Some people may feel uncertain or awkward creating recognition certificates if they're not used to doing it. Make it easy for them by taking a few minutes — in a meeting or one-on-one — to help them gain familiarity with any software, stationery or certificate materials you have assembled for your program. And, be sure to give them a reward for taking on this new task!

PART III

Summing up...

- *Praise presents social acknowledgment, while a reward bestows a tangible award – for best results, strategically combine the two*

- *Choose awards that fit your corporate culture and the people you work with*

- *An award certificate commemorates achievement in a memorable, personalized format*

Ten winning awards
- Gift certificates
- Money
- Merchandise
- Personal service
- Entertainment
- Benefits
- Travel
- Time off
- Lunch or dinner
- VIP parking spot

Make It Happen

Develop a central design for individual application

The 'decentralized' approach

Within large corporations and organizations with many branches, award incentive programs often take a decentralized approach, with each branch or department "doing its own thing." Each site develops its own standards, measures, goals and rewards.

On the one hand, this decentralized approach ensures more timely reward presentation, more personal awards and less hassle with sifting through bureaucratic red tape. Total control is in the hands of management within the various locations. The program can be flexible and easier to administer. Because they deal directly with people and their performance, managers are in a better position to reward extra-mile efforts and understand extraordinary circumstances.

Take care that your decentralized approach doesn't create an atmosphere where "the right hand doesn't know what the left hand is doing." Managers in different areas reward similar work with dissimilar rewards, causing confusion, and perhaps contention, among employees of all areas!

Priceless Words

"Managers are not athletic coaches; they do not need to motivate for a short-term burst of supreme effort but for a long-term streak of sustainable effort."

Saul Gellerman, Ph.D.,
Motivation in the Real World

The 'centralized' approach

Centralized programs, designed to be administered company-wide, use the same goals, measures and rewards for the same results. Though implemented at each location, a central directive dictates the planning and structure of the award incentive program.

One benefit of centralized planning, common goals — established company-wide — present a valuable opportunity to unite staff members. Common standards of performance excellence can foster teamwork among various sites and departments. As you put your program in place, make sure bureaucratic red tape doesn't interfere with your spontaneity in rewarding your star performers.

The best of both worlds

If you opt for a centralized award program, include some options for spontaneity and individuality within your plan. Encourage your managers to give verbal recognition, on the spot, to people who are performing admirably. Urge them to hand out personalized certificates for *Extra-Mile Performance* or *In Appreciation*. Put up a bulletin board in each location where award winners are listed the day managers submit their names to the corporate office for recognition.

If the decentralized approach seems more your corporation's style, make sure managers compare notes on the *who, what* and *how* of their individual recognition programs. Set up a special award for managers having success with their reward program. Last of all, make sure each manager has good resources, both for learning about reward programs, in general, and for creating awards for the people in their departments.

Spread the word

Too often, when a recognition program debuts, managers make a big announcement and let it ride. They expect employees to "pick up the ball and run with it." This doesn't work. People don't believe in it. A prevailing wisdom states a person has to hear a new idea seven times before buying into it. Business author David Hanna tells us, "It takes three to five years to change a deeply entrenched bureaucratic culture." Just because you have developed a recognition program — even the most creative one around — employees may not be excited about it, believe in it or improve their performance because of it. They simply won't trust it at first. It takes time. If you expect employees to buy into your recognition or incentive program long-term, you have to sell it, sell it and sell it again.

Package your program

Think about how your organization sells its 'product.' What's one of the most important aspects? The packaging! Your recognition program is no different. Give it a name, theme and identity (maybe even coordinated graphics). Your program's identity can be a great rallying point for employees, giving higher purpose to their endeavors.

Three keys to naming your recognition program.

- Tie your program name to its goal
- Choose a name that reflects your organization's image
- Keep it short and simple

Recognition kits

Kathe Farris, recognition consultant for BankBoston, knew her biggest task would be prompting managers to make recognition a priority. After some training, she developed a pre-assembled "Recognition Kit" with recognition cards, a small book of tips, certificates, pins and a local resource list for other awards. The kits were very well received. Because she made it easy for managers to recognize others, the program was a success.

If you develop a program graphic, use it on greeting cards, updates, internal company communications, newsletters, certificates and as a logo on pins and awards. Your recognition program package doesn't have to be expensive. Use pre-printed papers and motivational merchandise, centering your theme around graphics that already exist. Then add your own touch to create a unique program for your organization.

Keep communication lines open

Communication is an ongoing process. Hold frequent meetings. Talk one-on-one. Circulate memos, newsletters and status reports. All of these show people that management cares about them as individuals as well as producers. In addition, frequent communication provides opportunities for managers and staff members to check their perceptions against reality. When a person or team receives an incentive award for good performance, those not meeting the mark may be surprised to find out they're not "on track." Good communication will prevent such surprises (it's the very backbone of a recognition program's success). People can't improve if they don't know what management expects from them. Communication proves even more important in eliminating uncertainty within organizations where people work on their own, with little staff interaction.

Accentuate the positive

Instead of focusing only on areas needing improvement, accentuate the positive. Praise motivates people and gives them a sense of self-worth. Think of motivation as being back-to-back: a pat on the back along with feedback. In other words, make praise a priority.

Negotiate the negative

When people don't produce the desired or expected results, frustration can set in. Don't give in to it. Keep your goal in mind. Take special care when communicating bad news or discipline, remembering improvement is more profitable than punishment.

Specifically state the substandard performance:
Instead of saying, "You aren't selling enough," say, "You need to sell more RK100s."
Explain why the performance is substandard.
Share how it affects productivity and performance.
Instead of saying, "You need to boost profits,"say, "Increasing our sales by 10 percent increases our profits by 20 percent. That means profit sharing checks will double."

Explain specific expectations or required changes:
Instead of saying, "You need more sales,"say, "If you make 10 more sales calls each day, we'll reach our goal."

Share the positive rewards that will happen when performance improves and the negative consequences that will result if it doesn't:
Instead of saying, "I guess we won't be giving out any profit sharing checks this quarter,"say, "If we pull this off and reach our goal, profit sharing checks will be $1,500 each. On the other hand, if we fall short of the

goal, our profit sharing will likely be only $350 each." Overall, let your message be, "You're okay. It's your performance that needs to be better."

Celebrate success

To be meaningful, celebrations should take place as soon after the actual achievement as possible. When you don't celebrate until the end of the year, when you don't make awards until "Recognition Week," when you wait until everyone is available, your reward will diminish in both meaning and impact. A celebration event should capitalize on the powerful, human emotions felt during the achievement, accomplishment or job well done. By being creative and timely with your celebrations, you keep people focused on their achievement and promote intrinsic motivation.

Inspire management to 'buy-in'

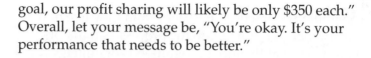

Though thoughtfully developed, creatively designed and easily implemented, your recognition program won't fly if management won't buy into it. Recognition is a cultural issue. While it does start with one person — and one person can make a positive difference — for organization-wide success (improvement in individual attitudes, general morale and performance profitability), recognition must pervade throughout the entire organization. Everyone has to buy into and be a part of the process.

Joan Klubnik, author of *Rewarding and Recognizing Employees*, said that recognition is a pulling strategy. When recognition is practiced on people and they like how it feels, they get pulled into the process as initiators. It has to start at the top. Recognition is definitely a trickledown, contagious phenomenon. The more it's repeated, the more it spreads.

Five pointers to inspire management buy-in

1. Tell them why it is important
2. Have a recognition plan to present
3. Ask for commitment
4. Give them specific action steps
5. Provide recognition materials & tools to get started

Your organization's size will determine your strategy

Small company? Start at the top

If you work for a small organization, recognition has to start at the top. The owner or president should initiate the program and take an active role in the recognition process. When employees see commitment from the top, they'll "get with the program" a lot faster. In small companies, owners may believe people feel appreciated and valued because they work together so closely. Not so. Usually, the dynamics

Priceless Pointer

A Caveat… don't overdo! Save praise for when the accomplishment merits it. When over-used, praise loses its power to motivate.

Part IV: Make It Happen

of a small company require workers to perform several different duties, some in areas where they are skilled, others where they are not. By recognizing what people are doing right and providing feedback on what needs improvement, owners can instill self-worth and motivate peak performance. People in small organizations crave acknowledgment and appreciation just like everyone else.

Medium-sized business? Head for middle ground

Medium-sized organizations often experience the most flux. They're not small anymore. They're not big yet. Their people must deal with a lot of uncertainty and change. In such an organization, both top and middle management must declare their commitment to the recognition program. People see recognition coming from their immediate supervisor or manager as most meaningful. Since mid-sized firms give people regular access to the top, senior management must display an element of understanding and commitment to the program, as well.

Large firm? Make sure every name has a face

Within a large company, with all its complexities, initiating a recognition program throughout the entire organization can prove a daunting task. To get started, senior management must commit to the program. However, the program's success depends on the middle managers. In a large organization, recognition from some obscure VP working out of a different office will not feel nearly as meaningful as praise from an immediate manager. After training your middle managers about recognition in general (how to give it and why it's important), give them the tools for making the program work. Make it simple. Repeat the message of Priceless Motivation again and again. As the recognition advocate for your organization, you may meet some resistance (especially if your program represents a significant change). Carry on. Your organization, and the people within it, will profit from your dedication to the principle that "People Count."

Part IV:
Summing up...

- *Develop a recognition program that fits your organization's goals*

- *To get people to buy into your program long-term, you have to sell it, sell it and sell it again*

- *Package your program as attractively as you'd package your product*

- *Pre-printed papers and motivational merchandise can make your job easier*

- *Communicate your program via meetings, memos, newsletters and one-on-one conversations*

- *Work to inspire management buy-in*

Managing Motivation

Keeping the fleet upbeat

The rationales for implementing reward and recognition programs are basic: People count. People need praise. Praise improves performance. The programs we've outlined in this book are simple. However, a solid recognition program works best over time and with consistent effort. Corporate cultures evolve slowly, so make sure you cover all the bases:

- Inspire management buy-in
- Communicate the message of recognition
- Market your program
- Choose meaningful rewards
- Train managers to listen, look and recognize a job well done

Smooth sailing

When your program is in gear and going well — and people show excitement — you can coast for a while, but don't get lulled into a sense of complacency. Instead, take a deep breath, pat yourself on the back and get back to work. Make your recognition program work even better. Adapt it. Change it. Evolve it to fit your organization's unique mix of people and product.

Keeping people energized for the long-term challenges any ongoing recognition program. As a driving force, your program should instill positive work habits — not become one more chore on a to-do list. If you sense your program has become routine, make some adjustments.

Priceless Words

"I have faith that the time will eventually come when employees and employers, as well as all mankind, will realize that they serve themselves best when they serve others most."

B.C. Forbes

Part V: **Managing Motivation**

Priceless Pointer

One of the best known awards, the Oscar for Best Actor or Actress, confers a gold, engraved statue symbolizing excellence and success in acting. A major network televises this elaborate event during primetime; an aura of suspense and excitement surrounds the evening. Great symbolic value is attached to these coveted awards.

Somehow it wouldn't be the same if this year's Best Actor received a big screen TV. If your firm creates its own "Corporate Oscars," dignify and commemorate success with proper ceremony and awards befitting your event!

10 strategies to propel your program full-speed ahead

Stay focused
Remember your recognition program's importance.

Don't let up
Keep the momentum going with picnics, pot-lucks, ice cream socials, crazy tie Fridays. A break from business as usual can foster great enthusiasm.

Broadcast it
Post it on the bulletin board. Print it in the newsletter. Insert it in payroll envelopes. E-mail it to every computer. Write it with a friendly, little note. Announce it in meetings. Keep at it!

Innovate
Add a new twist to what you're already doing. Highlight different departments with "spiffs." Reward every error-free memo for a week, the department with best attendance for a month.

Track it
By documenting your program's progress, you can create rationale for continuing and note areas for improvement.

Show-off
If what you're doing works, other departments or locations should know about it.

More, more, more

Expand on what works. Help other managers or supervisors implement the program in their group.

Turn it up

After your program has run smoothly for a while, add activities, celebrations or periodic incentives.

Listen and learn

Poll employees. How do they suggest you expand or improve your recognition program?

Rally around a theme

For example, an Olympic "Go for the Gold" could include your own corporate Olympics.

Troubled waters

Your program looked good on paper. You trained some managers. Distributed some tools. Even bought the rewards. Then you waited, and nothing happened. Or worse — people got confused, problems arose, pandemonium broke loose. You're ready to jump ship — after all, the seas seemed calmer before the winds of recognition made waves.

However, you know that recognition is a powerful tool for positive change. When people are recognized for their efforts, they perform. When you have a plan in place for recognizing people and make it a top priority, people will get recognized. So clearly, a sound plan, soundly executed will bring success. Regroup. Go back to the basics. Keep your program afloat with a few fresh ideas.

Priceless Proof

To teach and reward teamwork, McDonald's sends selected managers to Corporate Cowboys, a dusty replica of a wild west town. Through paint-ball shoot-outs, rival "gangs" learn to work together as a team.

"Shoot-outs in Name of Teamwork"
Chicago Tribune,
Monday, April 29, 1996

Priceless Proof

- *By flying in a V-formation, a flock of geese can fly 71% farther than if each bird flew on its own.*

- *According to Success Magazine, in 1985 U.S. business spent $10 billion energizing workers with incentives. That figure has more than doubled to $22 billion in the last ten years.*

- *Rewards fall into two categories: cash and non-cash. The American Productivity and Quality Center's report, "People, Performance & Pay," summarized the results of a nationwide survey on nontraditional reward systems. The data showed that non-cash awards provided a higher return on investment than cash by almost three-to-one.*

10 strategies to keep your program on course

Clarity

Make sure your message is clear.

Comprehension

Make sure people understand your message. Even if it's clear to you, it may not be clear to others.

Simplicity

If you have a formal program, make sure it's simple. Too many rules or criteria can cause confusion, and people will simply ignore the program.

Feedback

Seek feedback from managers and employees.

Training

Many managers need to be shown and told how to praise and recognize effectively (they may never have received recognition themselves).

Tools

Assemble recognition kits filled with post-it notes, cards, certificates, how-to guidelines and other rewards for spontaneous recognition. Make it easy for your managers. Put the tools at their fingertips. Don't require requisitions.

Give your program a facelift

Create a new theme, new guidelines, new rewards and additional opportunities for recognition.

Recognize people who practice recognition

We all crave praise.

Incorporate the outrageous

Shut down for the day and take your staff outlet shopping. Arrange for a celebrity to stop by and sign autographs. Send the whole crew to a theme park.

Ask for outside advice

A recognition consultant can evaluate your program and suggest additional strategies to take your program to the next level.

What motivation will mean to your company

Now you know… of all the responsibilities central to the success of a manager, recognizing people's accomplishments can be the most important. If you're the person behind the scenes advocating your organization's recognition program, keep on the lookout for opportunities to promote your program.

Envision yourself as a one-person public relations firm responsible for publicizing your staff's efforts. Others may ask you, "Why all this effort? What will be the benefits?"

You know the answers. Don't engage in a vicious cycle of criticism leading to poor performance, low self-esteem, anger, bad attitudes and more poor performance. Instead, initiate a priceless cycle of motivation. Soon you'll see the people you work with feeling better about themselves and performing better for your organization.

Motivated people are productive people. People who feel good about themselves try harder. People who try harder get

Part V: **Managing Motivation**

Priceless Words

"Fail to honor people, and they will fail to honor you.

Lao Tzo, 600 B.C.

the job done. Continuing success fosters continuous improvement — and the achievement of excellence.

Excellence in performance will ensure your organization's success, while helping the people within your organization find satisfaction in their work and in their lives.

Thousands of books, seminars and consultants have offered magical motivational solutions. Organizations around the world realize the benefits to be gleaned from motivated, energized, enthusiastic workers.

Motivating people can seem an insurmountable task. But it's not. You've got the know-how. Make your plan. Invest in a few tools. Then simply recognize and reward the people around you. Keep spreading the good news. In time, fresh attitudes and a friendlier morale will enhance your organization's productivity, profits … and people.

People count. When you live by this premise, you also find out you can count on them. Motivate people by showing you value them; they will return the favor ten-fold with energized efforts. This simple concept gives you the power to redefine your organization. And that makes motivation truly priceless.

Part V:
Summing up...

- *Corporate cultures evolve slowly – try to cover all the bases*

- *Inspire management buy-in*

- *Communicate the message of recognition*

- *Market your program*

- *Choose meaningful rewards*

- *Train managers to listen, look and recognize a job well done*

- *People count, people need praise, praise improves performance for your organization*

Priceless Post Scripts

Interesting Award Titles: Serious

Grand Production

Outstanding Dependability Award

The Power of One Award

ENCORE AWARD

SILVER LINING AWARD

Priceless Performance

Supplier Key to Quality Award

You Are Our Best Kept Secret

Grace Under Pressure Award

Fanfare! Award

Behind the Scenes Award

Make a Positive Difference Award

Believe and Succeed Award

Standing Ovation Award

INFORMATION TECHNOLOGY EXCELLENCE AWARD

Attitude is Everything Award

Brilliance Award

Professional Excellence Award

Win from Within Award

Cost-Effective Solutions Award

ON TIME DELIVERY AWARD

Whatever it Takes Award

Stellar Proposal Award

Teamwork Plus Award

110% Solution Award

ABE LINCOLN AWARD FOR LEADERSHIP

Interesting Award Titles: Light Hearted

Rookie of the Year

High Five! Award

Thumbs Up! Award

The Invisible Man Award

Superstar

Top Dog Award

HATS OFF AWARD

Bravo!

Trust Your Crazy Ideas

PennyPinchingPerformanceAward

You are a Shining Star

Applause! Applause!

Ms. (Mr.) Congeniality

MVP

Just Did It Award

The A Team

Woman Extraordinaire Award

'Bee's Knees' Honey of a Bzzziness Deal Award

High Hurdler Award

Top-Drawer Tidy Award

Elbow Grease Award

Picture of Health Attendance

WHY DIDN'T I THINK OF THAT?

Your Halo's Showing

Miles of Smiles Award

Faster than a Speeding Bullet Award

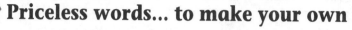

Priceless words... to make your own

Some people just don't know what to say. They want to recognize people, but they go "blank" when trying to be clever, witty or uplifting. The following is a sample list of possible short, positive messages that could be handwritten or spoken. Tailor your own personal message to suit the people and performance goals in your organization.

- Your personal commitment to quality is obvious in everything you do.

- Not everyone is a creative thinker... but you are.

- Your dedication to seeing a project through is second to none.

- Your dedication contributes to our success.

- You've got a winner's attitude. Of course! You are a winner!

- Your desire and willingness fuel our mutual efforts and lead us to success.

- Few people have your vision. Thank you for showing others an alternate perspective.

- Your ability to recognize and react to opportunity results in personal and mutual success.

- The service you provided exceeded all expectations, and guarantees a continuing successful relationship.

- Your ability to accommodate, even when it wasn't easy or convenient, assures others of a continuing, enjoyable, successful relationship with you.

- Your personal commitment to excellence has inspired others to push past mediocrity. They are changed because of you.

- Your dedication has shown that you can't ride an elevator to success — you can only take steps, one at a time.

- We recognize and appreciate your dedicated efforts.

- All achievements begin with an idea. Your innovations put those ideas in front. This impetus has empowered the momentum for success. Thank you for providing us with powerful ideas.

- When others were ready to admit failure, you steadfastly persisted. By refusing to fail, you contributed to the eventual success.

- Thanks for coming to bat at the end of the ninth inning!

- You wisely said, "I think I can. I think I can. I think I can." And, you did!! Congratulations!

- You faced many obstacles on this project. The way you negotiated them inspired all who worked with you.

- The new insight you provided was the greatest victory in the effort!

- Your healthy perspective on what is truly important inspires all whose lives touch yours. Thank you for making us stop to "smell the roses."

- Each exchanged idea and every shared opportunity magnifies the mutual respect we have for one another.

- Your ability to listen to others' ideas with concern and an open mind creates an environment of mutual respect where relationships flourish.

- You took the time — and that has made all the difference!

- It's your careful attention to detail that makes you so special.

- You consistently "go the extra mile."

- When others rush headlong into new undertakings, you remain mindful of the finishing touches that make a good job a superior job.

Part VI: Priceless Post Scripts

- Thank you for taking the initiative. Success can never be achieved unless someone, like you, has the vision and desire to initiate it.

- Your objectivity sets you apart from other leaders, and makes you easy to share ideas with.

- Two thumbs up! Your achievement is the direct result of your dedicated effort towards reaching your goal.

- Your extra effort, dedication, insights and opinions are all extremely valuable to the successful undertakings of this organization.

- Your personal pride in your work is obvious… and never taken for granted. The quality you attain is an integral part of our success.

- What a great idea!! Thank you for sharing it with us!!

- Your "whatever it takes" attitude has made all the difference in this effort.

50 Reasons to recognize

1. For the smile that's always there
2. Hands that are always willing to help
3. A creative idea
4. Consistent quality work
5. Continuous improvement
6. An extra-mile effort
7. Meeting the goal
8. Surpassing the goal
9. A winning attitude
10. Support
11. Loyalty
12. Punctuality
13. Cost-conscious behavior
14. Being part of the team
15. Solving a problem
16. Commitment to the customer
17. Service with a smile
18. A "whatever it takes" philosophy
19. Strong leadership
20. Having the vision to make it happen
21. Perseverance
22. Big dreams
23. For being fast and efficient
24. Making the commitment
25. For doing everything that's asked... and then some

26. Accepting a challenge
27. Seizing the opportunity
28. Overcoming insurmountable odds
29. Doing it right the first time
30. For believing and then succeeding
31. For "never quitting"
32. Being committed to the safety of others
33. Thinking ahead
34. Being a tactful manager
35. Managing time wisely
36. Motivating others
37. For having superior skills and ability
38. Having the courage to push ahead
39. Always expecting to win
40. Outstanding achievement
41. Making tough choices
42. Staying well-read and informed
43. Overcoming fears and failure
44. Always giving of time and effort
45. Ethical behavior
46. Being committed to team efforts
47. Accepting responsibility
48. For attendance
49. For blazing new trails
50. No reason at all

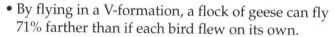

Priceless Proof

- By flying in a V-formation, a flock of geese can fly 71% farther than if each bird flew on its own.

- According to Success Magazine, in 1985 U.S. business spent $10 billion energizing workers with incentives. That figure has more than doubled to $22 billion in the last ten years.

- Rewards fall into two categories: cash and non-cash. The American Productivity and Quality Center's report, "People, Performance & Pay," summarized the results of a nationwide survey on nontraditional reward systems. The data showed that non-cash awards provided a higher return on investment than cash by almost three-to-one.

- To teach and reward teamwork, McDonald's sends selected managers to Corporate Cowboys, a dusty replica of a wild west town. Through paint-ball shoot-outs, rival "gangs" learn to work together as a team.

"Shoot-outs in Name of Teamwork"
Chicago Tribune, Monday, April 29, 1996

- When British Columbia Public Service employees contribute ideas and suggestions, they receive cash awards. Of note, these topics are not eligible for consideration: (1) personal grievances, (2) personal matters of classification and pay, (3) duplicates of an idea for the same office submitted within the last year, (4) matters beyond the scope of the organization, and (5) suggestions with costs exceeding potential benefits.

Internet Source

- 83% of medium to large companies have recognition programs and many have three to four programs in effect. Of those polled, 47% use non-cash rewards; 38% combine cash and non-cash; 15% use cash only. Common areas of recognition included service (59%); going above normal job requirements (51%); customer service or satisfaction (41%); saving money (39%); and improving productivity (37%).

William M. Mercer, Inc.
Spring 1996 survey of 213 medium-to large-sized companies.

Pricey problem...

- Managers today spend 13% of their time resolving staff conflicts, up from 9% five years ago. In other words, they spend six and a half weeks a year as the workplace's peace-keeping force."

Priceless solutions

- Eastman Chemical Company launched its Eastman Performance Plan by placing 5% of every employee's pay at risk. This gave employees a potential bonus of up to 30% of their annual salary — based on the company's financial performance. The first 5% of any annual payout was channeled into the employee-stock ownership program.

"Motivating For Success"
Sales & Marketing Strategies & News
May 6, 1997

- It takes three to five years to change a deeply entrenched bureaucratic culture.

David P. Hanna

- Elgin's Custom Aluminum uses pay-for-performance wage incentives. The plan pays bonuses for surpassing productivity and quality levels. Improvements are translated into dollars and shared equally between employees and the company.

  The Business Journal
  August, 1997

- Houston-based Continental Airlines recently held a raffle for employees with perfect attendance over a six-month period. Seven of the 12,000 employees won a Ford Explorer. The remaining employees were awarded airline tickets and gift certificates.

  Vincent Alonzo
  "Driving Down Absenteeism"
  Incentive Magazine

- Whirlpool Corporation of Benton Harbor, Michigan, instituted the Performance Management Process in 1989. The company bases annual payouts on a combination of corporate performance and individual employee performance.

  "Motivating For Success"
  Sales & Marketing Strategies & News
  May 6, 1997

- A study of broad-based incentive compensation plans in 475 major business organizations indicated that close to 50% of the participants employed individual incentive plans. Among those, 77% reported employee relations improved with their reward program; 50% reported more favorable business results.

  Hay Group/Business Week Report
  Nancy Austin
  The Service Edge
  Working Woman, July 1992

- If you wait to correct a problem until the next stage in a process, the cost of fixing it goes up ten times.

  W. Edwards Deming

- A behavior has to be repeated 17 times before it becomes believable to others!

  Natasha Josefowitz
  Paths to Power

- According to Hewitt Associates 1994 and 1995 Salary Increase Survey Report, spending for incentive programs is increasing, with employers budgeting an average of 6.5% of payroll for awards in 1995 up from 6.4% in 1994 and 5.9% in 1993.

  Incentive Magazine
  December 1994

- Incentives Motivate!

  Among respondents to a poll…
  66% would work harder with an incentive;
  79% might work harder;
  and 5% wouldn't work harder.

  Incentive Magazine
  November 1994

- Success days have a distinct emotional pattern characterized by high levels of feeling pleased, happy and cheerful.

  Personal Selling Power
  University of Michigan Study

Priceless Props

Putting applause on paper...

That's Baudville's specialty. When you're ready to implement your recognition program, feel free to give us a call at **800-728-0888** for advice. We'll be able to recommend easy to use products to get your program up and running.

Catalog Contents

Our catalog features 40 pages of software and paper for recognition, team building, and special events. Whatever you need for your recognition program--from award papers and certificate folders to fun and energetic border papers, cards, and coupons--you'll find it in our FREE catalog!

Use the **Recognition FUNdamentals Software** to print handsome, energizing awards; motivating, memorable coupons; and original, one-of-a kind mementos on the spot, with your computer and your inkjet or laser printer.
The software also *includes all the artwork you see in this book:* more than 50 pieces of clip art formatted for use in all your favorite desktop publishing programs.

When you want to kick off your recognition program with a big splash, or want to infuse your existing program with some new life, you'll want the **Recognition FUNdamentals Kit**. Including a sampling of recognition greeting cards, motivational coupons, Pocket Praise notecards, post-it notes, and more; the Recognition FUNdamentals Kit will help put your recognition program into full swing.

Part VII: Priceless Props

Start your program right...

Put together a stand-out recognition program that meets your organization's individual needs. The **Recognition FUNdamentals Kit** has the plan and the products to make your program an award winner.

The **Base Kit** Includes:

- Priceless Motivation idea book
- Recognition post-it notes
- 72 Reward coupons (includes 6 topics)
- 60 Pocket Praise Notecards
- 12 Greeting cards
- 60 Super Job! Seals

ITEM #	DESCRIPTION	PRICE
92395	Recognition Base Kit	$59.95

The **Deluxe Kit** includes everything in a Base Kit plus a FUNdamentals Paper Sampler and Recognition FUNdamentals Software CD-ROM at a savings of $40.

ITEM #	DESCRIPTION	PRICE
92428	Recognition Deluxe Kit	$99.95

Recognition FUNdamentals Software

Create your own coupons and awards quickly and easily with our new software. Paper Sampler ($24.95 value) and *Priceless Motivation Clipart* included.

ITEM #	DESCRIPTION	PRICE
12422T	Recognition Software CD-ROM	$79.95

Greeting Cards

Features a 12 pack of our "Team Guys" doing what they do best – motivating, and encouraging. Four different designs with envelopes included.

ITEM #	DESCRIPTION	PRICE
72420	Card Assortment	$14.95

Recognition Post-it® Pack

These friendly little post-its give you a quick and meaningful way to express your appreciation.

ITEM #	DESCRIPTION		
22375	Recognition Post-its (Six 50-sheet pads)		
1-4 PACKS	**10-29**	**30-59**	**60+**
$9.95	$8.95	$8.45	$7.95

Reward Coupons

Each of these motivational coupons has space for you to personalize. 72 pack includes 6 different styles.

ITEM #	DESCRIPTION	PRICE
72419	Coupon Assortment	$8.95

Super Job! Seals

Beautiful embossed foil seal with rich metallic blue ink. Sold in packages of 60.

ITEM #	DESCRIPTION	PRICE
62307	Super Job! Seals	$9.60

Pocket Praise Assortment

Spread goodwill wherever you go! 60 per pack.

ITEM #	DESCRIPTION		
72466	Appreciation Cards		
1-9 PACKS	**10-39**	**40+**	
$15.95	$14.95	$13.45	

Order Information

QUANTITY	ITEM NUMBER	DESCRIPTION	PRICE	TOTAL

Michigan Sales Tax
Michigan residents add 6%
or tax exempt number. _____

Shipping/Handling
Billed on all orders.
Minimum $6.95 _____

TOTAL AMOUNT _____

Shipping/Billing Information

NAME

COMPANY

SHIP TO ADDRESS

CITY	STATE	ZIP

BILL TO ADDRESS (IF DIFFERENT THAN ABOVE)

CITY	STATE	ZIP

PHONE	FAX	EMAIL

Method of Payment

☐ MasterCard   ☐ AMERICAN EXPRESS

☐ VISA   ☐ DISCOVER

EXPIRATION DATE
☐ ☐ ☐ ☐

CREDIT CARD NUMBER
☐☐☐☐ ☐☐☐☐ ☐☐☐☐ ☐☐☐☐

_____ SIGNATURE

Purchase Orders _Fax_ your purchase order with completed order form to 616-698-0554. For first time orders, please allow an additional 48 hours to open an account.

Check/Money Orders Call 800-728-0888 for shipping charges. Make check payable to: _Baudville, Inc._ Mail completed order form and payment to: Baudville, Inc., 5380 52nd Street SE, Grand Rapids, MI 49512.

**To order: 800-728-0888 or www.baudville.com**